WHERE IS MY STATE?

by Robin Nelson

first step nonfiction

Lerner Publications Company · Minneapolis

I live in a **state.**

A state is a piece of land
in a country.

The country I live in is the
United States of America.

My country has 50 states.

A state has many towns
where families live.

A state has cities, **suburbs**, and the country.

There is a **border** around each state.

I can find my state
on a **map**.

A family can live in a state in the mountains.

A family can live in a state
on the **plains**.

A family can live in a state
in the desert.

A family can live in a
state by water.

A family can live in a state by the Arctic.

A family can live in a state
in the middle of the ocean.

Where is my state?

My state is in my country,
where I live with my family.

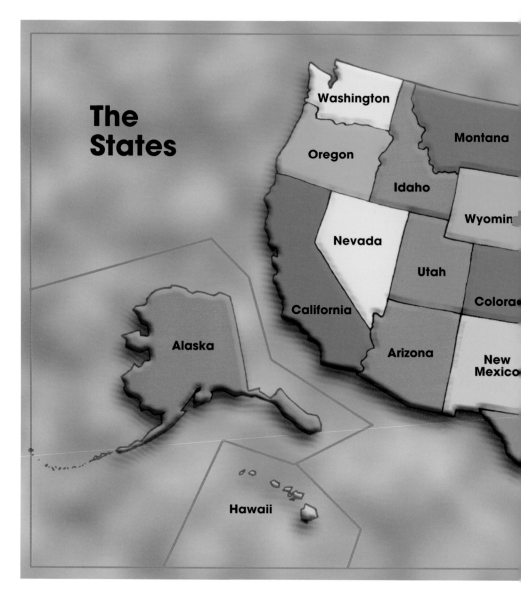

The States

Washington

Oregon

Montana

Idaho

Wyomin

Nevada

Utah

California

Colora

Arizona

New
Mexico

Alaska

Hawaii

Minnesota

North Dakota

Wisconsin

Michigan

Vermont

Maine

South Dakota

West Virginia

New Hampshire

New York

Massachusetts

Rhode Island

Nebraska

Iowa

Pennsylvania

Connecticut

New Jersey

Indiana

Ohio

Delaware

Illinois

Kansas

Virginia

Maryland

Missouri

Kentucky

Oklahoma

Arkansas

Tennessee

North Carolina

South Carolina

Texas

Georgia

Florida

Louisiana

Alabama

Mississippi

State Facts

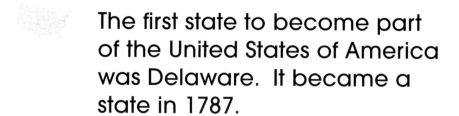

The first state to become part of the United States of America was Delaware. It became a state in 1787.

The last state to become part of the United States of America was Hawaii. It became a state in 1959.

The biggest state is Alaska.

The smallest state is Rhode Island.

The state with the largest number of people is California.

The state with the smallest number of people is Wyoming.

In the United States, the 50 states are divided into 7 regions. These regions are New England, the Middle Atlantic, the Southeast, the Southwest, the Midwest, the Rocky Mountains, and the Pacific Coast.

Glossary

 border – an imaginary line between one area of land and another

 map – a drawing of an area showing borders, towns, water, and mountains

 plains – large, flat areas of land

 state – one of many areas of land that make up a country

 suburbs – areas on or close to the outer edge of a city